GETTING BACK TO BASIC VALUES:

A DOZEN PLANS FOR HELPING

A Dozen Plans to Help Yourself and

Others Get on with Life!

Steve J. Leatherwood, MA, LPC, NCC

Sidney B. Simon, Ed.D., Professor Emeritus, U-Mass

Based on the original work of Dr. Louis E. Raths, (1900-1978)

Professor Emeritus, NY University

FIRST EDITION

Vol. 2

Cover Design by CreateSpace Cover Designer

Distributed by Amazon Books

ISBN-10: 1543011470
ISBN-13: 978-1543011470

DEDICATION

We would not be able to do or write about any of this work if it were not for the efforts of Dr. Louis E. Raths, N.Y. University, Professor Emeritus. His work in the 1960s and early 1970s brought meaning to the concept of personal and family values and our need to make what we value part of our daily lives. Dr. Raths' early writings included: "Meeting the Needs of Children: Creating Trust and Security"; "Teaching for Learning", "Teaching for Thinking: Theory, Strategies and Activities for the Classroom" and "Values and Teaching: Working with Values in the Classroom" (written with Dr. Sidney B. Simon). These early works sparked an interest in personal development, personal growth and values education that continued to thrive for decades.

We believe that this early work and teaching had a major impact of the lives of individuals who experienced it at that time. Over the more than forty years since this initial work, however, it appears our world has lost focus on personal values and caring for and about others and special parts of their lives. We have moved from generations who cared for each other, to self-centered and un-caring populations and even to generations doing intentional harm to others.

This series of books is dedicated to reviving the work of Dr. Raths and others which needs to be part of our current living, learning and acting. It is our hope that other individuals will take an interest in re-forming and re-dedicating self to values and to teaching family values, caring and love for one another. In this way, just maybe our world can, in fact, become a peaceful and loving place to live again. If we don't take an interest soon, the chance to save our world may be lost forever.

Please accept our warmest and best wishes for an exciting journey in self-discovery and learning. And, allowing a great philosopher to have the last word:

"The unexamined life is not worth living".

Socrates

GETTING BACK TO BASIC VALUES

TABLE OF CONTENTS

PREFACE AND FORWARD

This series of books is based in some of the work of Dr. Louis E. Raths, educator and professor emeritus at N.Y. University. His work began quite some time ago in the 1960s and 1970s. This work triggered an awareness of "values" and the importance of "values" in people's lives. It also triggered others to begin working and developing materials related to values education in schools. Dr. Sidney B. Simon was one of those people and in the early 1970's, he published several books about values and values education. "Meeting Yourself Halfway", "Negative Criticism", "I.A.L.A.C", "Vulture" and others, worked to explain how we sometimes hurt ourselves and others with our words and actions but also how we can learn to replace hurtful words and actions with VALIDATIONS: caring and loving words and behaviors.

This series is a compilation of some of the work from over 40 years, updated to fit today's world along with some new thoughts and ideas to complement that early work from the 1970s. We have had such fun re-thinking and re-defining this valuable work. We hope that you can appreciate its importance as much as we have come to appreciate and use it in our lives, families and careers.

This work is timeless and has as much, and even more, ability to impact individuals and families today as it did in the mid-1970s. The plans and ideas included in this book and series are meant to be used by individuals and groups to raise awareness on value issues, challenge participants to look at what they do value and work toward standing up for and strengthening their personal and family values.

Honestly, for a time, people were frightened to talk about 'values', thinking someone would 'teach' people the WRONG things to value. Nothing is farther from the truth, however, since people are more likely to "catch" values by watching what others do and say than be taught them in a classroom. Personally assessing and forming a strong and clear set of things of value is at the core of a mentally healthy person. And, mentally healthy people help to raise mentally healthy children, perform mentally healthy tasks and work to improve the mental health of their world.

It is our sincere hope that you will read and work with this material in that fashion, building and strengthening your personal and family values and teaching others to do the same. We may have slipped away from the 'old fashioned values' once present in our lives, but we can get back to that simple and solid foundation of caring, loving and respecting ourselves and others.

Best wishes to you in your journey to greatness.

Sid and Steve

PLEASE ENJOY THE RIDE!

WE CERTAINLY HAVE!

INTRODUCTION: WAYS TO USE THIS PLAN BOOK

Our PLAN BOOK is meant to be used much like any other, one plan at a time. And some plans, you may use often as you consider yourself, work with your children and family or even as you work with clients and others.

Some of the plans and ideas are meant to be ways to introduce members of a group to each other, some are meant to probe your thoughts for ideas and answers to a question and others are meant to help your organize your thoughts and ideas into plans and solutions.

Several, you will use over and over, like 'Brainstorming' or 'the Planning Board" since these are like 'tools' you might use in **any** situation where tools were necessary. Some are intense but powerful and you may use them repeatedly for building relationships and making decisions.

We hope that you will use the covers off this book and put these thoughts and plans in place to help yourself, your family and friends as well as your clients grow and develop positive and effective values and lives where those values can thrive. When we "value" health, relationships, self and other similar things in our lives, we grow to be stronger and more caring individuals, parents, partners, friends, and workers.

People, who love themselves and others, tend to avoid harming others and work toward building healthy relationships and loving and caring connections with others. We sincerely hope YOU and those around you can benefit positively from the plans and ideas we have to share.

Let's get started !

1 - NAME TAGS

This particular plan is one we have used countless times to begin the process of working with a group of individuals. This can be used with adults, children, adolescents or a mixed group of all ages. The aim of this plan is to build a climate of trust and respect for the other group members. It is designed to be used with groups of individuals who have never met but it is also great for groups who may know each other but who have never truly 'met' the other person, only know them by name or face. Sometimes this is the case with individuals working together daily or even family members. Often times, we "pass like ships in the night" and really learn or know little about each other more than a face and a name or job title.

The plan involves giving each person a large 5x8 or 6x9 inch index card they will use to create a "name tag". If you have time to prepare early, a great option is to punch 2 holes in each card, thread a long string or piece of colored yarn through the holes and tie it off at the ends leaving enough string to pass over the person's head and hang around their neck. If time is limited, paper clips or safety pins will work too.

The ultimate goal is to invite the members of the group to really know the others at a deeper level, even though they may be acquainted. They may know where others go to school, work or live but most often it is superficial knowledge. This will add more meaningful and personal information to 'being known' by others.

Have the participants draw a DIAMOND shape longwise on the card, touching the middle of all four sides and leaving four distinct triangle 'corners' with the large diamond in the middle. This provides FIVE specific areas for writing or drawing information. Think of the corners as numbered from 1-4 with 1 being the upper left and moving clockwise around the card so that 2 is the upper right corner, 3 is the bottom right corner and 4 is the bottom left corner. And, of course, there is the large diamond is in the middle.

In the middle LARGE diamond, have the participants write the name they like to be called, and would like the others to use for them, at least for today. This can be their real name or a nickname they like but a single name is enough like "John" or "Buck" or "Susan". Under their name have the participants write the city and state where they live. Even if they are from the same area, they may live in small towns or even across state lines.

Now, with the FOUR corners. These can be used for a variety of bits of information but the plan calls for you to ask for information that generally will not be known by others even if they have met before. Here are some options as possibilities but you can make up your own depending on the group and your goals with the group. Specify a corner by number (1-4) as noted above so that the information will be in the same location on everyone's card.

1. In what city were you born?
2. If you had a chance to live in another state (city, country) where would that be?
3. What are three things you are really good at doing which most people don't know?
4. What are two things you would like people to say about you to others?
5. What do you hope to be doing FIVE years from now?
6. What person would you most want to be like (could be living or dead)?
7. If you could be somewhere special right now, where would you be?
8. What is the most fun place you have ever visited?
9. What was the happiest moment in your life so far?
10. What is something you would like to change about yourself?

Now, obviously there are too many options here. And these are only suggestions. Please consider your group and what your goals are and adjust your questions accordingly. This can also be used with younger children who can be asked to draw pictures or even paste in pictures if time will allow. Some optional instructions for younger (non-writers) might be:

1. Draw a 'stick figure' picture of your family.
2. Draw a picture of your pet or pets.
3. Draw a picture of something you like to do.
4. Draw a picture of somewhere you like to go on vacation or trips.
5. Color one corner your favorite color.
6. If you could be an animal, draw what animal you would choose to be.
7. Draw a face that shows how you are feeling right now.
8. Draw a picture of your favorite person and be ready to tell about them.
9. Draw your favorite shape (circle, star, etc.)
10. Draw a picture of your favorite food (especially one someone wouldn't know about!)
11. What is your favorite flavor of ice cream?
12. Draw a picture of your favorite sport or game to play.

Once completed have the participants put on their name tag (string or pin) and have them choose a partner (adults, usually pairs or threes and younger might do better in groups of 4-5). You can judge what works best in your situation. In this grouping, have the individuals share the information on their cards with each other. Time the process and allow 3-4 minutes for each (adult) and a couple minutes for each of the kids to share. When completed, ask participants to 'introduce' one of the other members in the pair, or small group by sharing some of the information on the person's card with the whole group until everyone is introduced.

Participants will wear the name tags throughout the workshop or time together as a way of knowing names and continuing to find out information and build relationships with each other. Your name tags might look something like this and you can make all sorts of variations on the theme as you wish to apply to your situation and needs.

NOTE: It is important to make sure that very sensitive information be avoided, such as information that might be difficult to share or that participants might not want to have known by others. Use good judgment in choosing your 'corner questions' so that no one feels singled out or put on the spot to tell something 'secret'.

MATERIALS LIST:

1) 5x8" or 6x9" INDEX CARDS

2) PENCILS/MARKERS IN COLORS

3) YARN and HOLE PUNCH (for hangers)

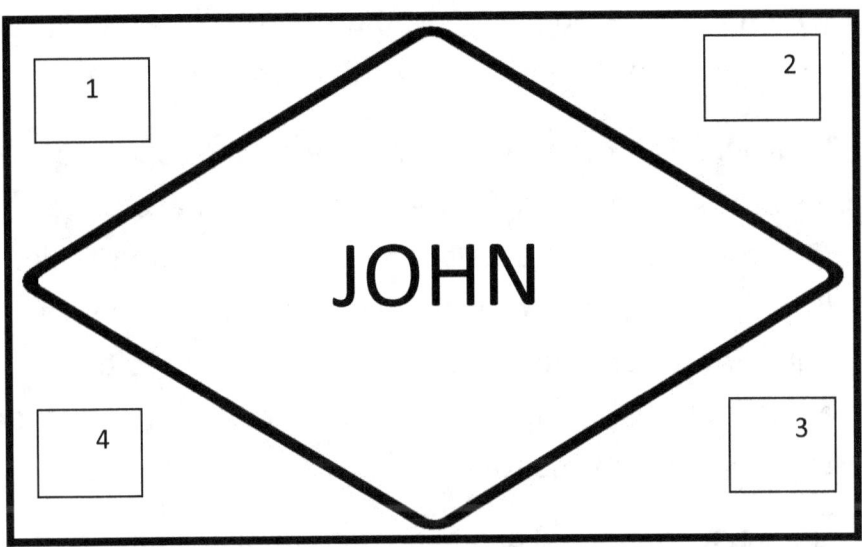

2 - BRAINSTORMING

This plan is probably one of the most simple but most often used in many exercises and other activities we recommend. It simply involves making a list, as quickly and creatively as possible, of all the things that come to your mind in response to a stimulus question or idea. Nothing is omitted at first. Write down everything.

Usually, this is used in problem-solving and especially in an intensive group discussion that does not allow a lot of time for research and reflection. The 'rules' are simple: list as quickly as you can, every thought that comes to mind. Ask everyone in the group (or you can do this alone, but usually, the more the better!) to say whatever they think about the topic.

No one is allowed to eliminate an option or say something like "that won't work" or "that's stupid" since often outrageous and impossible sounding options generate totally viable and perfect options for solving a problem or developing an action plan.

The key is to work as quickly as possible and don't block any thought. Write down everything anyone says. You can set a time-limit or simply go as long as you want until people run out of ideas.

Then, go over the list and mark out items that everyone agrees are not logical or practical. Maybe consider items that might take more time than is possible for the solution to be enacted. But eventually, narrow down the list to a number (we are thinking maybe a dozen) that might work.

Taking the final list, PRIORITIZE / RANK ORDER* the options and determine the top 3-4 ideas. Discuss the possibilities and limitations of the top options and pick the ONE idea that makes the most logical and reasonable sense as a solution to the problem. You may want to have 2-3 person small groups to discuss the options and agree a top solution.

It is a SIMPLE and POWERFUL technique. Remember, this plan is one you may use again and again in other situations. *You will learn about PRIORITIZING next!

simple

Getting back to the basics

3- PRIORITIZING and RANK ORDER

The Prioritizing or Rank Ordering plan can be used in many different ways and for many purposes. By name, it means assigning a 'priority' or a 'rank' to the items being considered. In this case, it is done for the process of elimination of some items and determining the most important ones.

There are a couple ways to work this plan. One simple way is to have the participant simply number the items (let's say 12) in order of importance from 12 to 1 (easier to start with bottom item!). Number 12 is the least important or bottom of the list and Number 1 is the most important. That's easy enough and will work well in a lot of listings you might do in other strategies and situations. The #1 thing is the most important and so on down the list. Every items will have only ONE place!

Here is a slightly more complex option using TWO groupings. A-B-C and 1-2-3 is used as a way of refining the order at a higher level. In this method, items are broken down into "A" items which need to be done first and are most important to be included. Then "B" items which are next in line of importance but can't be considered until all the "A" items are done. And finally, "C" items get done only if there is time, room or energy left to do them and sometimes they even become unnecessary during the processing of "A" and "B" items.

Now, don't forget the 1-2-3s either. Looking at the "A" items, while they are all the most important, SOME are more important than others, so they get 'ranked' 1-2-3 with number 1 being the most important and on down to 2 and 3 or more. Same with "B" and "C" items, some are more important than others and will be numbered like the "A" items with 1 – 2 – 3.

The theory behind this numbering and ranking system is to make sure that "A-1" gets done first and is followed by "A-2" and "A-3" and all the "As" get done before starting on the "Bs". Then "B-1", "B-2" and "B-3" but in order. You are not allowed to skip over and do a "C" item before all the "As and Bs" are done.

What happens sometimes is that energy, money, time or other resources are spent before all the tasks are done but if the MOST IMPORTANT ones are done first, in order, then the most important items DO get done!

Here is a simple example. My wife plants a garden and likes to grow as much as she can in her little acre plot. However, there are more things to grow than she can fit into the plot. So, she has to make a list which might include tomatoes, okra, green beans, peppers, corn, potatoes, watermelon, cucumbers, and squash.

Ok, that's 9 things she would like to plant. But she also likes to have a lot of tomatoes, peppers and cucumbers since those are canned for soup and made into pickles and canned. So, these are the "A" items. Tomatoes always rise to the top and become "A-1", peppers are usually "A-2" and 'cukes' would come in at "A-3". So she will need to allot the amount of space needed for the "A" crops and see how much room is left.

Then she will go to the "B" crops which would be green beans, okra, and squash. So, now we get okra in at "B-1", squash would slide in at "B-2" and green beans are "B-3". The little acre is filling up and not a lot of space remains. But, if there is room, "C-1" would probably be potatoes, "C-2" is watermelon and "C-3", corn. By the way, the "Cs" often get cut from the list and we have not grown corn or egg plant (we just buy them) in about 6 years!!!

Sometimes at dinner we play a game of ranking our TOP 3 Pizzas, TOP 3 movies, TOP 3 places to eat out and other rankings. This is a fun family activity and allows the whole family to get in their "favorites" and maybe be chosen at some point for the family outing or meal! We will use this as part of other plans along the way so keep it in mind as a helping tool.

4 - THE BAKER'S DOZEN

Most of us think of the "Baker's Dozen" as being ONE EXTRA, or 13, one more than a dozen. However, it didn't start out that way. The baker, about whom the story is told, was a 'stingy sort of fellow' many years ago who would actually give customers only 11 items when they ordered a 'dozen'. When he was threatened to have his hand cut off, he decided to become more generous and give an EXTRA item (12+1) making the buyers happy with 13 and bringing a good ending to the age-old story! And, he was able to keep his hand!

Anyway, in this plan, The BAKER'S DOZEN is a study on personal values, about what you really NEED in your life and what you could do without; or what might be unnecessary. And what is REALLY necessary. In this example, we will use HOME APPLIANCES for the 'items' to consider. These can be anything from stoves and refrigerators to irons, blenders, curling irons and electric toothbrushes, hairdryers and even televisions.

We could even think of this as an "energy saving plan" if you consider the electricity and energy some of these appliances consume. This can be stretched to include many other tasks and using all sorts of 'lists' of items.

In this case, make a list of 13 electrical appliances in and around your home. Things you frequently use and consider important and maybe some you think of as less important but you still use. REMEMBER: It's just a game but be serious!

1	2	3	4
5	6	7	8
9	10	11	12
13	XXXXXXXXXXX	XXXXXXXXXXX	XXXXXXXXXXX

OK, GOT THE LIST????

NOW, draw a line through THREE of the appliances you could probably, most easily live without and not miss after a while if you did away with them. Then, take a look at the ones left and consider their importance to you in your everyday life.

OK, NOW, getting TOUGHER, cross out with an X, **THREE more** that are the least important of the ones left. YES, it is getting harder, but that is the challenge. And remember, we are just 'playing' with this one so play along for a few minutes.

This should leave you with **SEVEN (7)** appliances that you consider the most valuable and necessary for your daily life. These should represent the 7 appliances you would hold on to as long as possible and not give up.

Now, let's use the RANK ORDER plan. Number from 1-7 (or 7-1) with 1 being the MOST important appliance you would really not want to give up and 7 being the LEAST important one you could give up if you had to give up one of the seven. Sometimes it is easier to start with 7 and work down to 1, but if you had to live by this priority, could you do that? Write in your TOP SEVEN below in RANK ORDER. Remember, #1 is the BEST!

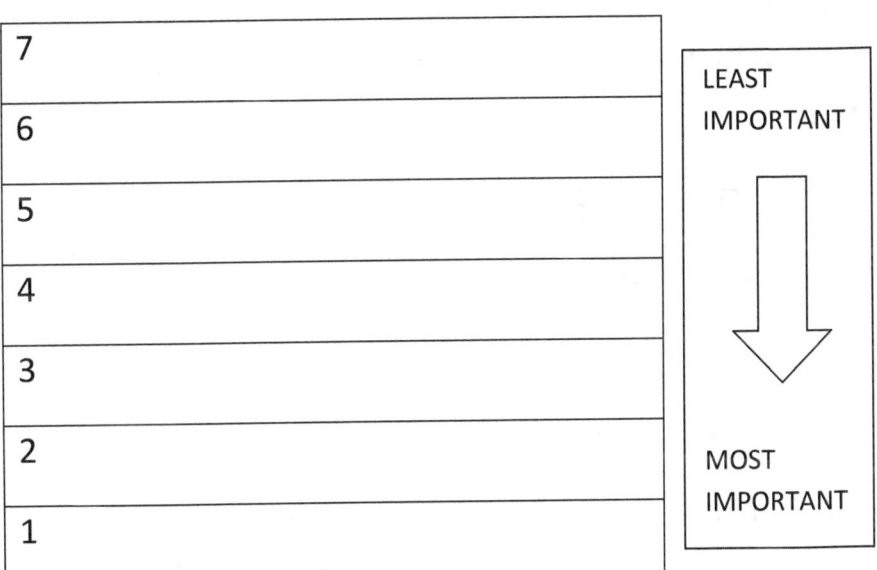

The BAKER'S DOZEN plan brings us up to the bare bones "things we just couldn't live without" and also about how much we depend on these items each and every day. Now remember, this is just playing with the concept of HOW IMPORTANT is something. BUT there may be times in our lives we **really** have to come to this level of decision-making about how much we REALLY need or WANT or CAN AFFORD something in our life. Then, the question becomes whether or not we would really be willing to let it go if we had to choose.

What if you made a list of other 'items' like television programs, cell phone time, social media time, clothing items, special foods, restaurants, eating out, cable television and so forth? We have often used this in classroom teaching and found, oddly enough, a few people could actually eliminate down to only ONE item they really had to keep!

The questions become:

> What CAN you live without?

> What CAN'T you live without?

> And WHY or WHY NOT?

I am reminded of the time at our house when we had a major snow and ice storm and a widespread power outage for more than two weeks. Large trees were down and took power lines with them. Everyone was with without electricity and struggling to keep warm, have food to eat, and missing other electrical items we normally had in our lives day to day. My two sons were without television!

We cooked on a small gas camp stove and heated water in our fireplace which provided heat for the house. We played cards or board games by candle and lantern light in the evenings. No computers! No television! No stereo! We did have some battery radios to get news about the storm. But not very much.

TERRIBLE, you might think. BUT, after the time was over and electrical lines were restored and we regained the television, and other appliances, it was unusual that we didn't seem to care as much about the TV or even the lights as we did before the storm. The boys often asked if we could just build a fire in the fireplace and make hot chocolate with water from the fireplace. And couldn't we just use the camp stove again, since it was really fun! And maybe we could even play board games by candle and lantern lights and turn off the electric lights.

There was less time on the computer and more time reading books, coloring, singing and playing piano and guitar and TALKING with each other! This was several years ago and I often wonder what would happen today in 2017, especially with all of our gadgets and social media, internet and other computer connections.

MAYBE, just MAYBE, it would be a good experiment today to determine what COULD we do without for a few days, a couple weeks or maybe for good? Would life be better, relationships be healthier and families closer for having to do some of the 'normal' things the HARD WAY? Our experience was before gas generators were very popular and many people have that luxury today. We didn't have one. But, honestly, I am glad we didn't. It was a wonderful experience for our family and we had a lot of fun.

Well that's the BAKER'S DOZEN plan. Do some serious considering about what you really, really need and how much of it you really need. You might be surprised and your family might take on a different look and feel. Enjoy your considerations and involve your family in 'thinking' about what you might 'LET GO' and live without. It can be a fun 'game' to play with the kids while at the same time helping them to realize they might, someday, have to make serious decisions in their own lives to have or have not when it comes to some things that might otherwise be considered necessary.

(Adapted from Meeting Yourself Halfway, Simon, Sidney B., 1974, Argus Communications, Niles, IL)

5 - THINGS I LOVE TO DO

Here is a simple but fun plan to do with yourself, your spouse, or family or as a discussion starter with a small group. Teachers can also use this effectively to start exciting discussions in classrooms. We have often used this as an 'ice-breaker' beginner plan in a workshop or as a fun, break from the 'hard stuff', and an enjoyable stimulation for a small group discussion in any seminar, workshop or training program.

It is as simple as it sounds. Ask participants to take a sheet of paper and number from 1 to 12 (we are still into the dozen thing!) although you can use any number that suits you. We have found that, in more recent years, participants in groups and even family members have a limited attention span so a smaller number will probably be more compatible with their willingness to participate. (We used to ask for 25-30!)

Give the whole group about 15 minutes to make their list but watch to see if people seem to be getting finished before that time. If you are doing this with your family, self or spouse, simply make your lists and move on.

There are a couple ways to process the list from this point based on the people involved. The idea is to RANK ORDER the list from 12 back to 1 (or whatever number you have chosen) with the goal of determining the number 1 thing you love to do. Granted, that may be difficult in that some of the things may be more difficult to do than others, may take more time than others or may be more expensive than others. But do your best to reach pretty clear rank order of the list.

Once you have RANK ORDERED the list, take the TOP 2 or 3 things on the list that could be done in one day's time and write a short paragraph story about a "perfect day" that would include all three things. If one or more of your TOP items are "all day" or multiple day events, take the ONE thing and write a story about a "perfect day/weekend" using only that one thing.

For a TOP THREE example, you might let's say, enjoy 1) cruising around in a convertible; 2) going on a picnic; and 3) having an enjoyable night with a loved one attending a concert and/or having a quiet dinner. Let's say too that you have the whole day off, a cooperative and available loved one to accompany you, access to a convertible and you can manage a quick picnic and dinner/concert plans. (A 'carry-out' restaurant pack is fine!")

If your TOP ONE item is a 'weekend cruise' then use that to describe your 'perfect day/weekend' being sure to add in the meals, entertainment, etc. that might accompany the cruise you have in mind. Again, let's say you have the weekend off, a partner to accompany you on the cruise and the money it might take to fund the outing! Remember, this is just a story so use your creative juices and have some fun with it. Keep in mind this is about YOUR PERFECT DAY/WEEKEND and may not be something you could do immediately but could possibly happen in the future.

PROCESSING:

A. If you are doing this alone, you now have a great plan for a day/weekend event that you can set in motion with someone you love and enjoy the fun, food, entertainment and companionship and whatever your plan includes. The deal now is to share the plan with the person you have in mind and pick a day/weekend!!!

B. If you are using this with your spouse or family, each person is asked to read their plan to the other(s) and share their perfect day so that the others in your family will have an idea what you REALLY would do in such a situation. The intent is to be able to share your ideas with the others in your family and maybe plan an event that would work for everyone involved and include elements from everyone's 'perfect day'. The children in a family can easily do this as well and will come up with their ideas which could be incorporated into a 'perfect family outing' where everyone gets some of what they want. It could also become a listing of multiple events or outings that would center on each person's favorite thing and the others could participate and enjoy.

C. If this is a plan being used in a group setting, have the group break into small 3-4 member groups and share their 'perfect day' with the others in their group. This will result in people talking about things they love to do and will reinforce the idea that it is possible to do things you love if you just set it up in the right way with the right people. Group members would be encouraged to take their story home and involve their family or others in doing a similar activity to plan a 'perfect day/weekend' for the family.

You could start your list here and rank your items on the left of the list.

RANK   A DOZEN THINGS I LOVE TO DO

_ ————————————————————————

_ ————————————————————————

_ ————————————————————————

_ ————————————————————————

_ ————————————————————————

_ ————————————————————————

_ ————————————————————————

_ ————————————————————————

_ ————————————————————————

_ ————————————————————————

_ ————————————————————————

_ ————————————————————————

YOUR "PERFECT DAY" STORY: (use other pages if you
need more space!)

6 - WHAT'S IN YOUR WALLET?

This is a quick and fun plan for use with your family at the dinner table or when you turn off the television or computer and spend some 'family time'. It can also be done as an 'ice-breaker' for group participation at a workshop or seminar but we recommend arranging the larger group into 3-4 person small groups.

Quickly, ask the people in the group to inventory a collection of things in their pockets, wallets, handbags or carry packs that say something about who they are as a person. It is important to do this quickly and not allow too much time for 'planning' anything, just do it quickly. 1-3 minutes is tops for the time.

Have the participants group the items into three groups: **P** for things from the PAST; **PR** for things from the PRESENT and **F** for things that have FUTURE use. Now, have each person in the small group share about the things they found and their significance.

For example, I did something like this earlier today with my key ring which I carry every day but I began to look at the things I was carrying. I found an OLD post office key that is no longer functional (and needs to be returned to the post office!), a couple keys to an old office that I no longer need, keys that I currently use for my car, office, house and other things, and a small pen knife with a screw driver, and other tools I use from time to time as the occasion arises. If I were to look further in my pocket, I would find a change holder that also serves as a safe place for guitar picks and various small items (and change!) like screws, bolts, paper clips, etc., I have found on along the way. And, couple receipts from the post office where I was mailing a couple packages.

Wow, that's a lot of stuff. But the point is, WHAT DOES THE STUFF YOU CARRY IN YOUR WALLET, PURSE, ETC. SAY ABOUT YOU? In the small groups, have each person tell a little about some of the things they found and why those things are or were important to them or why they will be important in the future. What do these things say about the kind of person you are? About things you value? About people who are important to you? About places you have been? About things you are doing?

We can learn a lot about ourselves and others simply by looking at what we collect in our pockets/wallets. I would also have an Auto Store discount card, probably some old receipts from a restaurant lunch and some expired discount cards for the local hardware store. Oh, yes, and some business cards.

In asking a person to talk about these 'treasures' in the wallet, we find out that they like to eat at a Mexican restaurant (old receipt), they frequent a certain Auto Parts store to buy parts and that they restore old cars. The couple guitar picks are there just in case of an opportunity to pick a guitar which says the person likes music and plays guitar.

In getting to know others, many people will tell you 'business and professional' things about themselves; things that SOUND good, but that is not who they REALLY ARE! In this simple exercise, we get to peek under the cover and see what this person is really like, what they do, who they are and what they REALLY VALUE. That is often much better to know than their job title! Sometimes it is quite surprising and fun to find out just What's In Your Wallet!

7- SLICE OF LIFE

The SLICE OF LIFE is a plan designed to take a look at just how much time and what part of our day or life we spend doing some regular activities like sleeping, eating, working, going to school or other activities. It is a direct and dramatic activity that requires the participant to DRAW a large circle or 'pie chart' on a piece of paper. This circle or pie represents the WHOLE day of your life. This plan can be used in groups or with an individual with equally successful results.

With the circle or pie drawn on the page (use a large, full sheet 8.5 x11"), have the participant divide the circle into quarters, straight down the middle from top to bottom and across in the middle from side to side. This makes FOUR equal slices and each slice is worth SIX hours for a total 24-hour day.

Now, have the participant consider the following questions and estimate time spent for each question. Have them write down an estimate (hours/minutes) for each question. If you are working with a group, it might be helpful to have a worksheet drawn up with the circle and the questions for each person to simplify the process.

1. How many hours do you spend sleeping on an average day?
2. How many hours do you spend working or at school on an average day?
3. How many hours do you spend doing work around the house on an average day?
4. How many hours do you spend with your family, including mealtimes on an average day?
5. How many hours do you spend with friends, away from your home or workplace?
6. How many hours do you spend working on hobbies, reading, watching television, on the computer, texting/emailing on the cell phone or on social media on an average day?
7. How much time do you spend alone with your spouse (if you are married) or with a friend?

Your approximate times and divisions of your circle or pie should add up to 24 hours. Now, divide up the pie or circle by marking additional lines according to your estimates. You can 'spice up the pie' by using colored pencils or crayons.

In recent years, it has become increasingly important to consider computer, social media and cell phone time as separate issues in the total picture as time here has risen dramatically. And the question might be, "Where did you get that extra time?" Interesting thought!

Again, as with other strategies, you are able to modify the questions to fit the circumstances and group with which you are working.

As a follow-up or continuation to this activity, you might also draw an "ideal pie" which would reflect ways you would **LIKE** to spend the 24 hours you have in a day. Maybe some of the pie 'slices' would change and others slices might be added.

Follow up statements are helpful in processing the activity. Ask participants to complete the following:

- I learned that I ....
- If I could, I would like to decrease the time I ......
- I would like to increase the time I ....
- I am sure my family would like for me to ....
- I didn't think about spending that much time ....
- I need to re-consider ....
- Maybe I need to stop ....
- My life might be easier if I ....
- My family relationships might be better if I ....
- I would probably be less irritable if I ....
- Others would probably like me better if I ....

And other such incomplete sentences. We decided to help you out with the 'circle' or 'pie' chart and draw one below. You can add in the details as you see fit.

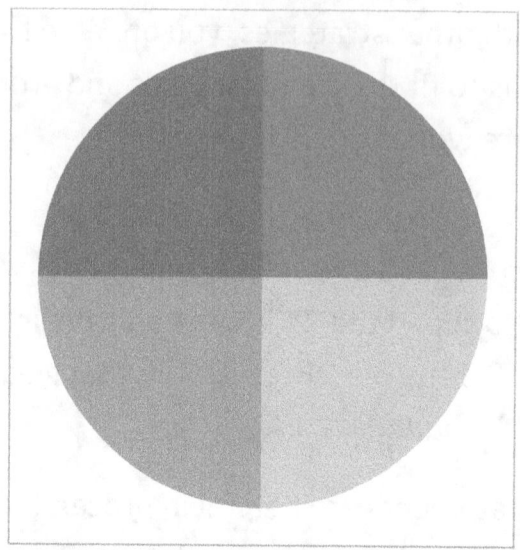

QUESTIONS: How much time do you spend......? (Make a note of the hours to the left of each numbered activity and add other ways you spend time.)

1. SLEEPING
2. WORKING/SCHOOL
3. FAMILY
4. ALONE
5. CELL PHONE/SOCIAL MEDIA/COMPUTERS
6. TELEVISION
7. HOBBIES/WORK AT HOME
8. FRIENDS
9.
10.

Actual "TIME CHARTS" will not be nearly as 'even' or equal as this one appears. (For demonstration purpose only.)

8 - LANGUAGE OF VALIDATION

In this plan, we would like to have you consider the 'way' you talk to others; your spouse, your children, your co-workers, other family members, etc. And consider how what you say to them actually sounds.

Many people are taught that it is very important, as parents or friends, etc., to point out when children or others make a mistake, say something wrong or do something that fails. Often, people are even trained to believe this is their JOB and that, in a very important way, they are actually helping the other person or persons to 'right their wrongs' and do better.

We would like to propose a 'new style of language' called the Language of Validation in which people actually 'turn the tables' on what they say to others and rather than point out the mistakes and failures, pay attention to and VALIDATE things the others are successful at doing. Sometimes, people think they actually do this most of the time, but we have found that the truth is most likely the opposite; in fact, most of us get far more negative comments than validations or positive comments in any given day.

Some studies regarding school classroom interaction place the number of positive to negative comments at 1:13, meaning for every ONE positive comment, a student (or students) gets THIRTEEN negative comments from adults. Now, in a teacher's defense, kids are often difficult to manage and especially these days! But, by calling attention to the 13 negative behaviors, the kids doing well and being appropriate are often overlooked or taken for granted. Would it be possible to gradually turn a classroom around and have it more under control if we could pay attention to MORE of the acceptable and desirable behavior and to LESS of the negative? It might be worth a test. No doubt, it could be difficult!

In this plan, we will be looking at a language that includes statement beginnings like this:

- "I like the way ....
- "I admire how you ....
- "I am proud of how you handled ....
- "I am pleased you ....
- "I am excited about your ....
- "I was so impressed when you ....
- "It was so nice to see you ....
- "I am glad you were able to ....
- "I love the job you did on ....
- "I celebrate the way you ....

In acting on the Language of Validation, you are asked to look for behavior in people (children or adults) you can call attention to verbally by completing one of the above sentences. You can probably think of other beginnings and that is fine. But, can you image the surprise of your child or husband or wife or friend when you 'validate' their effort? It would sound like this: "I admire the way you handled that problem with your sister." "I am impressed by the neat job you did raking the leaves!" "I admire the responsibility you have shown about your school work lately!" "I am glad you received the award for helping others!" and so on.

In no way is this intended to be a 'reward' or 'bribe' to get someone to act a certain way, but it is simply about calling attention to something in the other person worth noting and recognizing. Like having a 'ticket punched'.

EXERCISES: If you are willing, check out some of these exercises to see how this can work for you and others.

A. A PERSONAL VALIDATION LIST:

Make a quick list of 10 (or more) things you genuinely like about yourself. Post this list where you can see it easily like on the refrigerator door or bathroom mirror. Whenever you are near the list, read through it as a reminder of what a good person you really are. When you make the list, code each item with the number of years you have believed this to be true about yourself. Mark a star by the ones that have recently been affirmed in some way to you by others. Then, circle the ones you would really like to have someone else recognize in you.

WHAT I LIKE ABOUT ME	HOW LONG?	RECENT AFFIRMED?
1. SMILE A LOT	12 yrs	YES, Tuesday *
2.		
3.		
4.		
5.		
6.		
7.		
8.		
9.		
10.		

B. VALIDATIONS YOU WOULD LIKE TO HEAR FROM OTHERS:

Here is another exercise that involves others in your life. Take a separate piece of paper (or use the diagram below) and divide it into four sections. Write the name of a person important to you at the top of each of the four sections. Under the name in each section, list the validations, affirmations and encouragements you would like that person to say to you more often.

You can code these as well according to **how often** you would like to hear it, the date you **heard it last**, and put a check by the ones you think you might be able **to ask** the person to actually do for you. Granted, this is a little more difficult, but this is about changing communication patterns and developing communication that will enhance your self esteem and overall wellness.

Think of FOUR PEOPLE in your daily life, and start by writing their first name in the boxes of the next graph.

NAME	NAME
NAME	NAME

The challenge now is to share this list with the people noted in each square. Would it help if you did that?

C. EXERCISE FOR PARENTS OF CHILDREN: An Inventory

Use separate sheets of paper for each child. Draw a line down the middle of each page. On the RIGHT side of the paper, write the word VALIDATIONS and on the LEFT side of the paper, write the word CRITICISMS. Now, think about the last dozen things you said to your child or each of your children. Write down as many CRITICISMS and VALIDATIONS as you can remember in the two columns. Don't waste time feeling guilty or anything silly like that; just write down what you said. Check the RATIO: Criticisms vs Validations.   How does it look to you? Could you change the ratio tomorrow, next week, and maybe for a long time? Would it make a difference in the relationship you have with your child? Would it possibly bring about a positive change in a child's behavior? And, would it TEACH a more positive way to communicate with their own friends, family and children someday?

D. BIRTHDAY VALIDATIONS

Birthdays are such important events that validations need to be a vital part of the celebration. At the simplest level, just after singing "Happy Birthday" to the person, we recommend that individuals take turns to publicly say some aloud a validation to the birthday person. The person will glow with happiness and excitement upon hearing the validating words from others. Use the beginning phrases above or make up others but be positive and direct.

Another option for this exercise is to have those attending the party, dinner or celebration write validations for the birthday person and put them in a special box to give the person. This is especially helpful if a large number of people are attending or where some people who are less likely to talk openly about their validation. In addition, the birthday person will have the validations in writing to save and read over and over becoming a gift that never stops giving.

A twist on the writing of validations is to have people hide the validation notes around the house where the birthday person is likely to find them; sock drawer, lunch box, on bed pillow, etc. I suppose, you could even put one under their cell phone but that would be an easy find!

Given the role of cell phones in today's world, people could also write validations and text or email them to the birthday person. This is so much better that some of the messages we have seen that were sent out by bullies who were not at all nice. And these messages could be saved and re-read again and again.

In addition, a positive use of cell phones and email is to extend time you have or do not have with the birthday person. Remember, the VALIDATIONS are about positive qualities and attributes observed in the birthday person.

E. HUSBAND AND WIFE VALIDATION INVENTORY

This plan is similar to the Parent's Inventory only using husband or wife as the recipient of the communication. Use a separate sheet, draw a line down the middle of the page. On the RIGHT side of the paper, write the word VALIDATIONS and on the LEFT side of the paper, write the word CRITICISMS.

Now, think about the last dozen or so things you said to your spouse. Write down as many CRITICISMS and VALIDATIONS as you can remember in the two columns. Don't waste time feeling guilty or anything silly like that; just write down what you said.

Check the RATIO: Criticisms vs Validations. How does it look to you? Could you change the ratio tomorrow, next week, and maybe for a long time?

Would it make a difference in your marriage and relationship if you did some changing in the way you communicate? Practice some validations now!

HUSBAND-WIFE or PARENT-CHILD

INVENTORY SHEET

CRITICISMS	VALIDATIONS

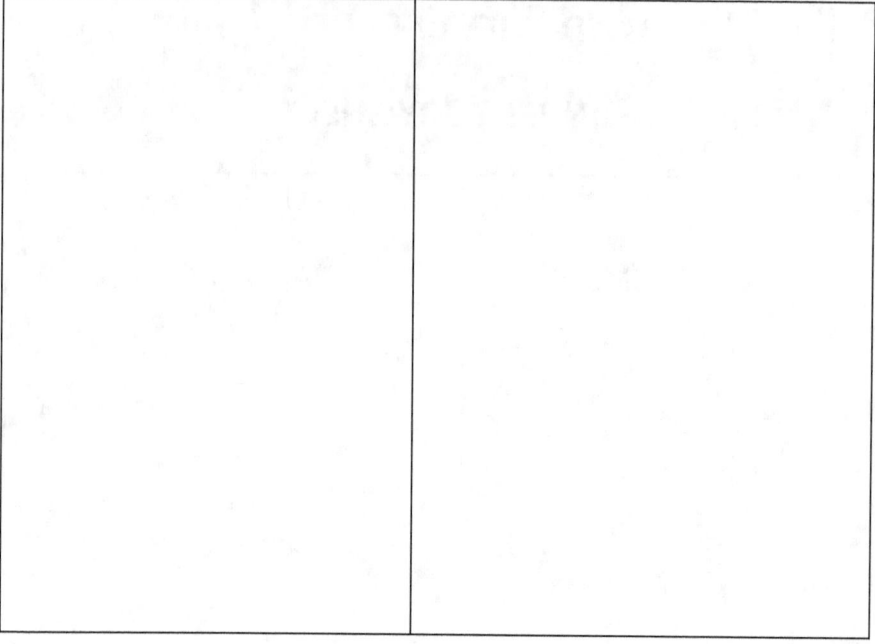

WIFE to HUSBAND (CHILD)   HUSBAND to WIFE (CHILD)

A good follow-up to this inventory would be to ask participants to write in the above columns, validations *they would like to hear from* their spouse or they believe their child might like to hear from them.

REMEMBER: A "Validation" is **NOT** a "reward" or a communication saying "If you will do this...., I will give you this..." it IS SIMPLY calling attention to something observed in the other person that is worthy of attention and "validation". It is intended ONLY to make the other person feel noticed for their efforts and appreciated by others. There is NOT a hidden addenda to change the other person.

PRACTICE SHEET FOR WRITING VALIDATIONS I MIGHT USE OR VALIDATIONS I WOULD LIKE TO HEAR!

9 - THINGS I RESPECT ABOUT ME

We have found that many people have been taught not to talk too much about themselves and their accomplishments; things they might respect about what they have done in life. They have been taught such behavior might be like bragging or attempting to make yourself look better than someone else.

This plan disregards that training as inappropriate and actually as harmful to one's self image. It is critical for individuals to understand they have accomplished things that are worthy of RESPECT. It is permissible to ask yourself at least, "What it is that I RESPECT about what I have done in my life and work thus far?".

So, take a piece of paper (or you can write in the book if you want) and as you consider what you respect about yourself, write down those things in a list. We ask that you get at least a DOZEN but if you think of more, please extend the list as far as you like. We would love to ask for TWO DOZEN but sometimes that is beyond some people's attention span these days.

As a college assignment in earlier years, we asked for students to come up with a list of at least 50! So do as many as you want. If you are doing this with others or as a couple, family or group, the same rules apply.

When you get your list finished, **PUT an A** beside ones that you respect yourself for doing alone; your personal accomplishments. **NEXT, PUT a T** by ones you accomplished working with a TEAM of others. And finally, **PUT A STAR** by the MOST IMPORTANT thing on your list that you want to be respected for by others; a kind of 'thumbprint'.

If you are doing this in a group or even within a family or couple, sharing your list and the 'special items' on your list would come next. In your own words, tell about how these particular accomplishments raised your level of respect for yourself. Remember this is not about putting someone else down, but about RESPECTING yourself for a job well done and worthy of recognition.

START YOUR LIST HERE!!!!

I RESPECT ME FOR:

1.
2.
3.
4.

5.

6.

7.

8.

9.

10.

11.

12.

Self-Inventory

10 - THE PLANNING BOARD

Probably one of the most useful tools in our work has been the PLANNING BOARD. This can be adapted to organize thoughts on literally any set of ideas or data. And you can use varying numbers of squares. For many years, we always used a DOZEN squares and I still like that number! But, here we will use only EIGHT! You can use any number that seems to work for your situation.

The planning board is simply a page with EIGHT (or more) empty squares. Participants are asked to make a planning board by folding TWO sheets of paper in half, long-wise making a long rectangle (both pages stay together). NEXT, ask the participants to fold the pages (still together) in half at the middle, each time creasing down the folds. Finally, ask them to fold the pages in half again and crease down the folds.

When this is done, have them unfold the pages, separate the two and lay one page to the side. Looking at the page, the folds should be obvious that the page has been divided into eight (8) equal squares; two columns of FOUR squares each. Have them take ONE sheet and tear it into 8 squares along the folds they have made so they have 8 small pieces of paper for writing.

When this is done, there should be ONE COMPLETE page with 8 squares (4 squares in 2 columns) and 8 individual pieces of paper in the same size squares. Most people will get this although it may require some assistance with others. If you want and have the time, you can also photocopy a 'drawn up' sheet with eight squares and cut up small squares to fit and clip 8 together for each participant. Lots of work for you, so really, we suggest the folding exercise using the participants as workers. It is also good to develop paper folding skills and following directions! You can also increase the number to fit your needs and have 9 or 12 but that is probably enough.

From this point, the planning board becomes a tool to RANK ORDER 8 options or alternatives or things you provide as part of a decision to be made. For example: we could take a list of 8 ways to spend your next birthday; 8 things you would like to do for a summer vacation; in fact, any 8 things you would like to rank order from 1-8, you make up the list.

Taking ONE item from the list at a time, have the participants place it on the blank 8 square planning board in one of the 8 blocks which are numbered 1-8 with top left being number 1 and bottom right being number 8. Number 1 is the BEST spot and most desirable position while number 8 is the bottom of the list and least desirable.

Say aloud the items one-at-a-time and have participants guess where they would put the item ranking it from 1-8 without knowing all of the options. They are free to move items around on the board, but only one item can occupy each space. They do place each item on the board without knowing all the other options.

Continue until all 8 items have been placed on the board in some location. Remember, NO SHARED spaces. Every item has its own place 1-8. Ask the person to review the board and make sure they are happy with the ranking. They are allowed to move items around until they are satisfied.

Next, ask participants to REMOVE item #8 from the board and then ask if they could be happy with just the TOP 7 items on the board. Have a show of hand of those who would accept the loss of number 8. Next, have them remove #7 and see if they would accept just the Top 6. Again, a show of hands.

Continue removing items one-at-a-time and see how far you can go until people are not willing to give up an item. Remember, it is important to make one of the items something really desirable to have for their birthday, Christmas, vacation or other event.

Several variations follow:

1. Have participants write a paragraph explaining why they would keep their top 3 or top 4 items and would refuse to give them up.
2. Have participants tell/write about their #1 item and what made it rise to the top.
3. Have participants organized the 8 items on the page for someone special in their life (spouse, friend, etc.) and write down their order THEN have that person actually do their arrangement and compare their results.
4. Have your family do this to determine the top 3-4 ideas that might be considered for a vacation or trip somewhere (this way everyone gets to speak for their favorite)

You can make up other options for use and certainly BRAINSTORM a list of things to be RANK ORDERED or PRIORITIZED on the PLANNING BOARD. It is a fun and powerful way of organizing options without having anything 'equal'.

Play around with it and you will have some fun. And, you will probably see us include this plan in other activities yet to be revealed.

11 - LIFELINE – RAINBOW PLAN

In recent years, it has been stressed to make lists of things you want to do within your life time; things to do before you die. This may seem like a grim sort of exercise but really it is about a celebration of life and living it to the fullest potential; doing and accomplishing the things we really, really want to do and accomplish. It is about planning to utilize every day to achieve some goal you have set or something you want to achieve.

On a piece of paper, draw a line across from side to side. Place a big dot on each end of the line. The dot on the LEFT signifies the day you were born so put your birthday under the dot. Now, the dot on the right signifies the date of your death. Over this dot, make your best guess how long you hope to live and put that year over the dot on the right. (Let's assume you take good care of yourself and this will be a long and productive life!) Take a look. This is your life on a line.

Now, place a third dot on the line that represents about where you are now on that line and write today's date above that dot. Sometimes this is a little frightening for us to see in black and white, but the truth is, it is reality and we have what we have, and we can make the best of what we have by planning and doing the things we really want to do. Does this life line represent a merry and happy life? A good life? A worthwhile and meaningful life? Well, let's hope that is true and work to make it so in the future.

To the LEFT of the dot that represents today, draw a half-circle under the line connecting it to your birthday dot. Inside the half-circle, write down some of your accomplishments to date. That might include graduating from high school, getting a job, buying a home, and other things which would certainly depend on your age and the position of the dot!

Then, to the RIGHT of today's dot, draw a large arc, like a rainbow, over to the dot at the end of the line. Now, under the rainbow, make a list of some of the things you really, really want to do before you die. Not to be morbid, just think about what you really want to get done. The rainbow side might include going to college, writing a book, learning to play a musical instrument, having some children, becoming a photographer, ... what else? The possibilities are unlimited; at least we have been told we can do whatever we set out to do. So, this is about making a list that you will set out to do – beginning today!

No more putting off or procrastination. No more excuses about not enough time or too many other things to do. If it is under the RAINBOW, it is important and has to be done! No EXCEPTIONS! Make a PLAN and GET STARTED! You could RANK ORDER the 'to do' list too!

This is about ACCOMPLISHMENTS and here that means making the most of yourself within yourself, within your own personal capacity to do, to make something happen. And, not surprisingly, it is a matter of VALUES; what you REALLY VALUE will get done.

Happy Life! Have a LONG and MERRY one!

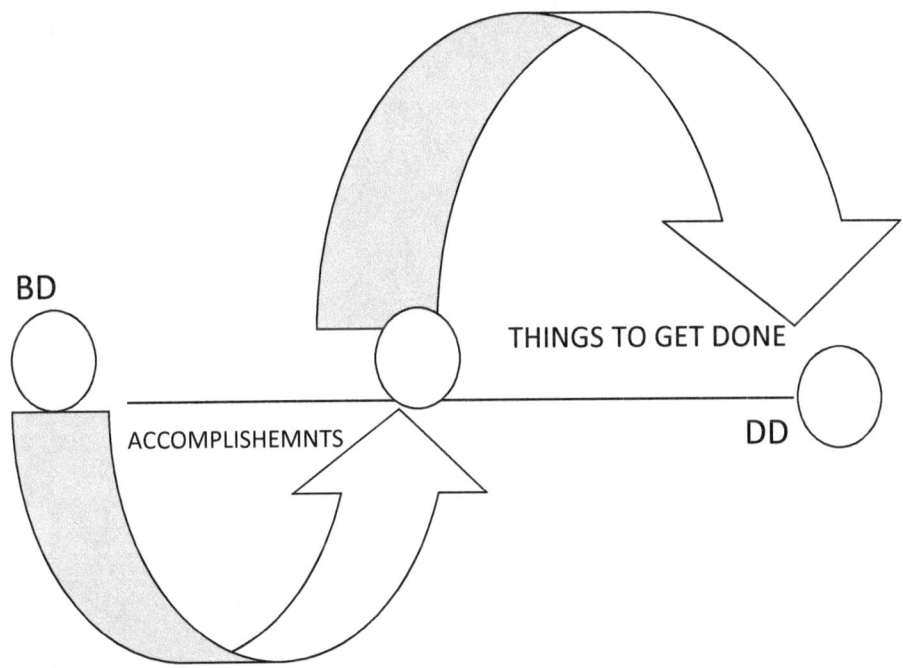

You can even use the next page to list MORE

MY "TO DO" LIST:

12- "VULTURE" – NEGATIVE SELF-CRITICISM

We have found that many people often spend too much time criticizing themselves or talking negatively to themselves about things they have done or the way others treat or have treated them. These negative words and perceptions damage the person's self esteem, even though many may not even be true or may have happened long ago. The person's memory of bad events, negative communications and failed efforts continues to pound away at the inner self. The actual source of the negative event may be long gone or may exist only in the person's mind but it continues to trigger the self put-downs and damaging thoughts over and over.

There are several known areas where these negative criticisms ("Vultures", we call them) seem to attack:

1. **Intelligence area** – WORDS LIKE: "I'm not smart enough; I'm just dumb; I can't do anything right; I'm just a failure; Nothing ever goes right for me; Everything I try to do ends up in a total disaster." Self talk that spins around and around in the person's head. It may be that someone or several others did say these things at one point, but they

became locked inside the person's head and continue to be remembered over and over.

2. **Family Relationships area** – WORDS and SITUATIONS LIKE: "I never get any positive comments from family; I always get fewer gifts; I never get as many birthday parties or invitations; My family doesn't even send me Christmas cards; Most of my family doesn't even care I exist." Sometimes, again, based in reality but maybe also just in perceptions. The person may be isolated from family and have difficulty attending family functions due to distance and travel issues. This gets projected into thoughts that the family does not want them around and never comes to visit them. It may be accidental on the part of the family as well if they are living complicated lives with work, children, distance and other issues.

3. **Social area** – THOUGHTS and WORDS LIKE: "I don't ever get invited to parties; Others are always talking about me if I do go somewhere; I am always the last one to be chosen for a team; If I do go somewhere, I just sit alone in the corner and no one ever talks to me." Social events are often bad situations for "Vultures" and negative talk to appear. It is difficult to make new friends

and if you feel negative about yourself already, it decreases your chances of meeting someone new who could possibly be a friend. In fact, the "Vulture" feelings and thoughts make it more likely people will have difficult approaching you and starting a conversation. "No one ever wants to talk to me anyway."

4. **Creativity area** – WORDS and THOUGHTS LIKE: "I never come up with any good ideas; I know everyone is better than me at doing anything; I just can't do anything special; I'm not creative at all." Maybe somewhere along the way, the person was told they were NOT CREATIVE and it stuck. Maybe they have failed in attempts to do creative things like draw, paint, play music, sing or write and they perceive themselves as lacking any creative talent. While this may not be the case at all, BELIEVING you are not creative actually makes it true since you choose not to attempt anything creative KNOWING you will most likely fail.

5. **Physical area** – THOUGHTS and WORDS LIKE: "I'm not pretty, tall, muscular, or slender enough; I'm just not "attractive" to others; I'm too THIN and ugly (television and social media help with this!); No one will even look at my social media page; I'm

too fat for someone to want to date." Many individuals are not particularly pleased with their physical 'looks' and will always dislike looking at their picture. We are taught by media that there is some desirable 'look' we should have in order to be accepted and liked by others. It is a prime target for "Vultures" and self put-downs.

The following exercises are for scaring away the VULTURES and forever getting them out of your life.

EXERCISES:

A. Make a list of the 'self put-downs' you dish out to yourself frequently (more than once a week). As you look over the list, 1) see if there are some you know are really NOT true. If you find one, mark it out and beside it or under it write how you REALLY feel that is a positive validation of yourself. 2) If there is another that may be somewhat true (poor hair style, never smiling, etc.) write down how you could REVERSE that one and make it into something you could feel good about and others would notice as positive. Treat yourself to a salon hair styling or practice smiling and laughing watching comedy programs. Begin to talk to yourself as if you are indeed a "smiling person" and smile at everyone you meet on the street. Don't overdo here, but at least LOOK happy (and you can do this even if you don't FEEL happy!).

B. Make a list of a couple things you could do to improve your self-image. If you are not doing creative things, think about what you might like to do and set out to learn about that thing. If you like cooking, you could take a cake decorating class or learn how to can and freeze your own foods. If you like working with your hands, but just don't know how to do some things, sign up for a small engine class or auto-body repair class at the local community college. You could take a computer class and learn more about computers since they are ALWAYS changing! Or maybe you could enroll in a music class to learn to play guitar, piano or some other instrument. Make a plan to turn your life around into one YOU will enjoy and others will notice in a positive way. The only problem is that if you don't make a plan and DO IT, you will fail. BUT if you make a plan and get started, you would probably be surprised how easily you could become a person YOU liked **and** others liked as well.

C. Consider joining some group, especially if you have even one friend who is a member of a reading group, coffee meet-up group or hiking group. If you have an interest, see if you can locate a few people who like the same thing. Sometimes a local church can be helpful with this and have a 'young singles' group. Or a swimming or exercise group at a YMCA. You might be surprised how many others are out there struggling in the same way you are struggling. It may be a little scary at first, but reaching out and being brave can get you closer to getting rid of the "Vultures" forever.

QUICKLY, write down as many thoughts as you can (brainstorm) about how you can scare away the "Vultures" and start putting together a new YOU that you can be proud to introduce to others.

START A DOZEN LIST RIGHT HERE:

1. SMILE MORE OFTEN (a starter!)

2.

3.

4.

5.

6.

7.

8.

9.

10.

11.

12.

BOOK LIST of VALUES

Kirschenbaum, Howard, *100 Ways to Enhance Values and Morality* in *Schools and Youth Settings,* Allyn & Bacon, 1994

Leatherwood, Steve J., *Choosing to Maintain Control of My Life,* Amazon Books, 2017

Raths, Louis E., Merrill Harmin, Sidney B. Simon *Values and Teaching: Working with Values in the classroom,* Merrill Books, Ltd., 1966

Raths, Louis E., S. Assermann, A. Jonas, and A. Rothstein, *Teaching for Thinking: Theory, Strategies & Activities for the Classroom,* New York: Teachers College Press, 1986 (First edition released in 1967).

Raths, Louis E., *Teaching for Learning*, Columbus, Ohio: Charles E. Merrill Publishing Co., 1969.

Raths, Louis E., *Meeting the Needs of Children: Creating Trust and Security,* NY: Educator's International Press, 1998 (originally released 1972).

Simon, Sidney B., Leland Howe, and Howard Kirschenbaum, *Values Clarification,* New York: Dodd, Mead & Co., 1972

Simon, Sidney B., *The IALAC Story,* Niles, Ill.: Argus Communications, 1973.

Simon, Sidney B., and Howard Kirschenbaum, *Readings in Values Clarification,"* Minneapolis, MN: Winston Press, Inc., 1973

Simon, Sidney *Meeting Yourself Halfway,* Amherst, Mass: Edit, Inc., 1974

Simon, Sidney B., *Carlng, Feeling, Touching,* Niles, Ill.: Argus Communications, 1976

Simon, Sidney B., and Sally W. Olds, *Helping Your Child Learn Right from Wrong*, New York: McGraw-Hill, 1976

Simon, Sidney B., *Vulture,* Allen, Texas: Argus Communications, 1977

Simon, Sidney B., *Negative Criticism*, Niles, Ill.: Argus Communications, 1978

Simon, Sidney *Getting Unstuck,* New York: Warner Books, 1988

Simon, Sidney and Suzanne Simon *Forgiveness,* New York: Warner Communications, 1990

OTHER BOOKS IN THIS SERIES:

GETTING BACK TO BASIC VALUES: Foundations for Helping Yourself and Others (Vol. 1)

GETTING BACK TO BASIC VALUES: A Second Dozen Plans for Helping Yourself and Others (Vol.3)

ABOUT THE AUTHORS

Steve J. Leatherwood, MA, LPC, NCC, began working as a psychologist at Western Carolina Center in 1970 following graduation from Western Carolina University with a BA in Psychology/Social Science. After obtaining a master's in Psychology from Appalachian State University and continuing post-graduate education in Greensboro, NC at UNC-G, Leatherwood worked consistently in the field of mental health counseling and psychotherapy. In the 1970's, he became Director of Psychological Services at Cleveland County Mental Health Center and was an adjunct professor of Psychology at Gardner-Webb University for thirty years. In 1975, Leatherwood met Dr. Simon and began conducting youth and adult seminars with Dr. Simon. In addition, Leatherwood has maintained a private practice in counseling and employee assistance programs since 1975. His focus for much of his career has been in working with children and adolescents, family and marriage counseling, personal growth and development workshops, and anger/anxiety management.

Sidney B. Simon, Ed. D. is internationally known for his pioneering work in Values Clarification, now retired as Professor Emeritus from the University of Massachusetts at Amherst, Mass. He has authored over 100 articles and more than a dozen books on values, self-esteem and personal growth and development and conducted many seminars and week-long workshops from Massachusetts to California. His work helped develop a set of practical strategies that have impacted counseling practice, education, social work, medical care and personal growth and development. Some of these strategies, plans and ideas are reprinted and up-dated in this series and other new plans and ideas have been developed for use and added.

YOUR PERSONAL NOTES AND THOUGHTS GO HERE

JUST FOR FUN!

SID at the beach!

STEVE acting silly!